MW01120547

VIRTUAL LEADERSHIP

VAL WILLIAMS

Virtual Leadership

Published by Shadowbrook Publishing
P.O. Box 2458
Edison, New Jersey 08818

First edition,

ISBN: 0-9712007-8-5

Dedicated to Jerry Noga, a leader who is committed to results and continuous improvement. Thanks Jerry for educating me on the challenges of "managing from afar."

CONTENTS

I. What is "Virtual" Leadership?

> **_Lead_** (verb): to be ahead; to show the way; to direct others to a result.
> -- Webster's Pocket English Dictionary
>
> **_Virtual_** (adjective): Being such practically or in effect although not in actual fact.
> -- Miriam-Webster

TODAY'S BUSINESS ENVIRONMENT

If you enjoyed science fiction as a kid, then you must love today's work environment. Cell phones, email, video conferencing, e-fax, teleconferencing, virtual relationships...!

In today's business world, we do a lot of business "virtually." It's <u>almost</u> like meeting people. You know their voices, you exchange products and services, you make deals and talk frequently, you feel you know each other...only you've never met face to face.

I have built a successful executive coaching business over the last seven years that is highly virtual. My personal assistant, Marie, is the best assistant I've ever had. She manages all my administration: invoicing, typing, checking email, mailing products, following up on voice mail, sending business proposals, scheduling, researching, even remembering to send flowers to my mom. I live on the East Coast, and Marie lives in the Midwest. And we have never met. She is a Virtual Assistant and she represents the new business environment. Business is done through technology these days.

In addition to having never met my personal assistant, I have never met many of my executive coaching clients. As a coach, I have worked with business executives from beginning to end to successfully strengthen their leadership and teambuilding skills, without ever meeting face to face! Sometimes we have worked together without meeting for several months; in a few cases we worked together without meeting for a couple of years.

So, over the last seven years I have learned some important lessons about working virtually. It takes specific skills and you have to pay attention, but virtual skills can be learned and applied to almost all business situations.

Virtual "leadership" is a special and very advanced skill. What is virtual leadership?

Virtual leadership is: "leading others to accomplish results in an environment that is other than physical."

Virtual leadership is managing direct reports in other geographic locations. Virtual leadership is leading a team of people who have never met. Virtual leadership is running an organization of dispersed people who are only connected by working on a certain project together.

Let's look at the challenges of virtual leadership. For example, you are a leader in a large organization. You work in New York but have direct reports regionally in

Boston, Washington, Chicago, Los Angeles, Seattle and Atlanta. They each have their own direct reports locally. You are responsible for national results. Before you even begin, here are a few of the challenges.

THE CHALLENGES OF VIRTUAL LEADERSHIP

*   ***Travel:*** How often are you going to have to fly around the country to meet your direct reports?

*   ***Relationships:*** How will you get to know them? How will you build rapport? How will you develop small talk about their personal interests?

*   ***Performance:*** How will you assess what kind of job they are doing? How will you evaluate their leadership skills? Their development of staff? Their results? When and how will you actually observe their performance?

*   ***Communication:*** How will you keep your direct reports updated? So much happens in a day; how will you have time to keep them in the loop?

*   ***Delegation:*** You don't even see them. How will you know who is capable of doing what? How will you track their deadlines?

*   ***Teambuilding***: They are dispersed. How can you build a strong team? They've never even met each other.

*   ***Email:*** You get hundreds of emails a week. How will you use email effectively to manage your staff?

- *Conflict:* With people so dispersed, how will you even know when you have a conflict with a direct report? Or when they have a conflict with each other?

- *Promotion:* How do you evaluate when someone is ready for promotion? Conversely, how do you keep from being "snowed"? How do you know when it's time to eliminate a poor performer?

- *Teleconferencing:* When will you have time for more long, boring teleconferences? (You hate teleconferences.)

- *Walking the talk:* In the old days, we did management by walking around. We showed people what we wanted by our own actions and body language. We "walked the floor." How will your direct reports observe you? See your style? How can you "model" if you don't see people?

These are only a few of the challenges of virtual leadership in today's new business environment. The old skills of yesterday no longer apply. Whatever got you promoted to this level probably worked fine when business was simpler.

Remember when you could actually walk down the halls and "drop in" on your direct reports? You could observe how they ran meetings; see them with subordinates, even sit in on difficult conversations. When you did their performance evaluations, you could list examples of things you personally observed. You

could look at their offices and notice if they needed more organization. You could see family photos or awards and be prompted to ask about their kids or hobbies. They dropped into your office or you went to lunch together to build a relationship. Remember all that? Leadership was pretty straightforward then.
Well, those days are gone.

Welcome to Virtual Reality.

II. Virtual Skills for Leaders

Virtual leadership requires a few additional tools in your leadership toolbox. When you are managing people or teams in diverse geographic locations, there are some new requirements.

The bottom line of successful virtual leadership is this: It is true that there are some critical differences in leading and managing people virtually vs. leading and managing people when you are in the same office. However, the most important distinction is that to successfully lead virtually requires that you become an outstanding leader. In fact, many of the key skills for leading virtually are the same skills that all exceptional leaders already use even if they do manage people face to face. So in some ways, virtual leadership is not so different. But it does mean that your leadership has to be very sharp.

For example, when leading people who work in the same office, a leader can sometimes get away with mediocre leadership skills and often still be fairly successful (at least short term). As an example, let's say the leader is not very skilled at "giving clear expectations when delegating." Well, if the direct report sits nearby, direct reports usually find ways to drop by the leader's office later and ask the leader informally for more clarification. Or the direct report may just happen to attend another meeting with the leader and get clarification that way. Or conversely, the leader may drop by the direct report's desk and notice he is on the wrong path and make a quick correction.

But none of that is good leadership. That is all lucky timing.

By contrast, when the direct report is in another geographic location, if the leader is not good at setting clear expectations during delegation, there is much less opportunity for informal course correction. The direct reports who are in another location are less likely to make a phone call or write an email to clarify (they could think it reflects poorly on their ability to be independent). The direct reports have no opportunity to "drop in," or to observe the leader informally. So the direct reports do their best and often the result is not what the leader wanted. The leader sometimes blames the direct reports and the direct reports blame the leader. The real blame lies in a lack of understanding that virtual situations require crystal clear expectation-setting conversations.

Following are three "Top Ten" checklists for the virtual leader:

- Top 10 Keys to Managing Performance Virtually
- Top 10 Best Practices for Coaching via Telephone
- Top 10 Keys to Leading Successful Teleconferences

If you manage people or lead teams in other geographic locations, you will find these key skills to be extremely useful.

Top 10 Keys to
Managing Performance Virtually

If you are a leader managing direct reports in different geographic locations, there are some key actions to take in order to do it well. Out of many successful actions you can take, these are the top 10.

1. **Have a formal discussion about work expectations.** This is just good management, but leaders frequently overlook this step when direct reports are in the same office. This is critical to do when you are managing virtually.

2. **Make clear agreements about communication style and format.** Decide with your direct report up front how often you want to be updated, at what level of detail and in what manner. What are your criteria for when to use email vs. voice mail?

3. **Have a formal discussion with your direct reports on benchmarks for successful performance.** Since you won't see each other often, agree up front on the types of deliverables you will need to get to know the direct report is doing a great job. What evidence? What benchmarks? When?

4. **Feedback on performance should be at least quarterly if not more often.** Virtual relationships break down very quickly without information flow. Some staff feel that "no news" is good news. Others feel neglected and unappreciated when the manager gives no feedback. All of this can detract from performance.

5. **Identify the actions you'll need to take in order to build rapport virtually with this specific person.** People are different. Assess each direct report individually. Some need a 2-minute phone call once a week where you chat about personal life. Others need only an email of recognition. The key is to make your actions fair across all direct reports but individual to the rapport needs for each.

6. **Coach people specifically on their objectives.** Learn at least five key coaching skills so that you can coach vs. manage people. There are many resources for learning coaching skills. As one example, see my book, *Get the Best Out of Your People and Yourself*, Chapter 6. Managing is difficult virtually. Coaching is easy virtually. If you can't coach, you can't lead.

7. **Use the Virtual Coaching Model.** Pulling together numbers 1, 3, and 6, remember the Virtual Coaching Model is:
   - Set objectives
   - Assess performance
   - Coach for action

8. **Ask direct reports for written self-assessments.** This will trigger feedback conversations and lay the groundwork for your coaching.

9. **Use face-to-face time well.** When you get together in person, get the biggest bang for your buck. How can you use "face time" to do things you could not do virtually?

10. **Ask your direct reports for feedback specifically on how well you virtually manage.** Let them teach you to be a better virtual manager.

Top 10 Best Practices
for Coaching via Telephone

1. **Pay 100% attention to the phone.** No email. No lunch.

2. **Listen with eyes closed.** Listen for tone, inflection, silence and pace of breathing.

3. **Match your behavioral style to the style of the person.** What is their style of communication? (For example, the DISC is one of many work-style assessments a leader can use.)

4. **Don't worry about missing body language.** It's true that body language can be a helpful tool, but if you strengthen your listening skills, you will be effective anyway. In fact, sometimes we can miss the essence of a person's message while trying to read body language. Body language can sometimes take away from listening.

5. **Phone coaching requires asking more questions to check out where a person truly is.** Ask lots of questions.

6. **Be fully present.** Therefore, to prepare, have your self handled: be well fed, rested, have your own tasks completed.

7. **Practice this high level of listening in all interactions, not just phone coaching.** Practice when there is no pressure.

8. **Have outstanding phone equipment and optimum surroundings.** Use a good-quality head set if possible, and make sure that you are situated in a quiet, confidential space.

9. **Use your intuition.** Feel for your inklings. Feel for the energy of the person you are talking with. What does your gut tell you?

10. **Have the person be comfortable and prepared.** Have the person prepare by sending a brief written checklist on what you plan to discuss. Have the person include the issue they are facing and how they think you can help.

Top 10 Keys to
Leading Successful Teleconferences

It is amazing how many teleconferences are boring, long, and waste a lot of people's time. This is a result of only one factor: poor virtual leadership. Here is a facilitator's checklist for running a lively and useful teleconference.

1. **Select a strong virtual facilitator.** The facilitator of the teleconference is not necessarily the leader, but could be. The key is to have a facilitator who is excellent in the real skill of "facilitating" vs. lecturing or managing. Someone who has good group dynamic skills, language skills and asks great questions.

2. **Set ground rules at the top of every teleconference.**
   - Say your name each time you speak.
   - Use your mute button if there is any background noise.
   - "Laser" your comments. Keep them short.

3. **Have a definite agenda**. Have the facilitator keep the group on the agenda and on time.

4. **Identify up front the desired outcomes for the teleconference.** Agree with the participants on what deliverable you all want at the end.

5. **Give feedback to participants (as a group).** Tell the teleconference participants what they did well on the call and where they need to shift. Do this halfway through if the call is not going well, or at the end if things are smooth.

6. **Protect everyone's self-esteem.** As the facilitator, it is your job to protect the self-esteem of every person on the call. Facilitators are objective. Do not criticize anyone. Do not allow others on the call to attack anyone. Do not allow others on the call to "hog" the air time.

7. **Intervene immediately where necessary.** A good facilitator will gracefully, but firmly, intervene if a participant is not following the ground rules. *Example: "Thanks, Sally. That's a good comment. Let's note it for later since it's not part of the agenda for this call."*

8. **Maximize group input.** Be sure to get everyone involved. Ask yourself: Are you as the facilitator helping the group truly interact? Or could what is happening have been summarized in an email? Be sure that whatever is going on in the call really required everyone's attendance.

9. **Debrief at the end.** Find out what participants got out of the teleconference. See how well it matched the agenda and intended outcomes and deliverables.

10. Evaluate before planning next teleconference. Who really needs to be there? Can this be done by memo vs. teleconference? Why not? What would be the purpose of additional teleconferencing? Make sure it is worth everyone's time.

Tips for Effective Virtual Oral Presentation

1. **Tone and Inflection of voice:** tone should fluctuate and not be monotone.

2. **Volume of Voice:** strong leaders have good volume to their voice.

3. **Speed of Voice:** hesitations in speaking make a leader sound tentative.

4. **Confidence:** your voice should communicate confidence.

5. **Check for Understanding:** when speaking on a teleconference, be sure to check in with the audience frequently. For example, "does what I just said make sense?"

6. **Laser It:** speak concisely. Get to the point.

Using Email to Coach and Lead

In order to use email effectively for virtual leadership, you have to really get the distinction between two words: "effective" vs. "efficient." Email is very efficient. It is quick. It is easy, and people can send and read email at a time that works for their own personal schedules. So yes, it is very efficient.

However, email is not always effective, meaning email does not always achieve your intended goal. The reason is that email has many unique shortcomings. Email is clear because it is written and in black and white type. However, email does not effectively convey tone or inflection. Email is therefore very easily misunderstood by the reader.

For example, think of times when you get an email labeled "URGENT." Before you even open it, you feel the adrenaline surge and sometimes the automatic resentment like, "What is this? What's so urgent?" Then the email is asking you to do something ASAP. But it does not feel like a request. It feels like someone is ordering you to do something with no regard for your schedule. Don't they know you are already over-worked?

And worst of all, the email makes it clear that the writer is not waiting for your agreement. In fact, it seems the person who wrote the email feels their job is done just by sending it, even if he or she has no idea of when or even if you have read it. Email—ugh!

So you are a leader and you have an appreciation for all of the above. How can you use email effectively to coach and lead your direct reports? And to manage upward and sideways to your boss and your peers?

Here are a few suggestions:

Email Tips

- **Laser it**. Become a master at short emails. Keep your email as short and to the point as possible. Executives at higher levels have no time or interest in long, detailed emails. Learn the skills needed to present your request or information in concise, bulleted format.

- **Create criteria for email.** Particularly with your direct reports, as a leader, you will need to create criteria for when an email is appropriate vs. a phone call or teleconference or in-person meeting. Have a specific discussion with direct reports on how you would like to use email as a team.

- **Agree on email etiquette.** Just as we have teleconference etiquette, most organizations are in dire need of email etiquette. There is no ultimate right or wrong on how to use email, but there are agreements people need to make. For example, one organization I coached had the following email guidelines for their own team:

- **Don't use all capital letters in email.** It's considered yelling.

- **Do not assume your email was read immediately.** People travel without email at times. If you need it read right away, add a voice mail.

- **Wait for agreement to an email before considering email complete.**

- **Be more thoughtful about who gets copied on emails.** Be able to state the reason someone is copied and include that on the email.

- **If you say an email is URGENT, it had better be! (the team actually defined "urgent").**

- **Do not use "reply all" unless all are truly interested.**

- **The team agrees on a reasonable response time for email vs. voice mail.** For example, 48 hours for voice mail, 72 hours for email (or whatever the specific team agrees on).

EMAIL COACHING

Although telephone is usually more effective for coaching, email can be a good adjunct. But remember, the phone is live. Telephone allows you to hear tone and inflection and know immediately what a response is. Email lacks that. Email is a time-delayed communication. A lot can change in business between the first email and the response.

However, there is a coaching industry called "cyber coaching" in which professional coaches do coach by email. So we know it can be done and done well. Here are a few easy suggestions that do not require the more extensive training that cyber coaches get.

- When emailing a direct report about a project, make your email a response that forwards the action. How does what you communicate spur your direct report to the next step?

- When coaching by email, ask lots of questions. But ask yourself as a leader, "Are your questions worth answering? How can you frame a question in a way that your direct report 'grows' just by trying to answer your question?"

   For example: **You run Operations. Your direct report is frustrated with the sales group and is recommending implementing controls to prevent the sales guys from selling products they have trouble administering. When you get your direct**

report's email with the recommendations for how to stop sales, you could email back. "Good recommendations, do it."

That's a totally valid response. But to make it more of a "coachable moment," another possible email response from you could be, "Good recommendations. How can we get sales on the same page with us so that we don't have to stop them?" That very question invites a different type of thinking. The direct report has to envision, be creative, and develop a strategy for the future vs. just complete a task in the present. That's coaching.

- Other ways a leader can use email effectively:
  - Communicate your vision for the organization to everyone frequently.
  - Copy the team on achievements of team members.
  - Keep the team updated on strategic direction.

- Email is NOT effective for:
  - Negative feedback on individual performance.
  - Conflict management.
  - Sensitive issues.
  - Very complex issues.

For the above, pick up the telephone or set up a face-to-face meeting.

SPECIAL CHALLENGES OF VIRTUAL TEAMS

When you are managing a "virtual" team, you will probably spend much of your time on the phone with the total group, or individually with group members. When you, as the leader, are on the phone with the total team, you have a wonderful opportunity for "group coaching," coaching the whole team together. Here are some suggested solutions for successful group coaching:

Top 10 Best Practices
For Group Coaching

1. **Group coaching means dancing between 2 skills: facilitating and coaching.**

2. **Prepare:** Time the agenda of a call: the flow, questions for discussion, live coaching, debriefing.

3. **Design the group:** do we have a specific topic or direction that we are coaching members on? Or, are we coaching members on whatever issues they bring to the group?

4. **Use the mastermind principle.** Group coaching is synergy. Tap into the knowledge and creativity of the entire group.

5. **Be spontaneous.** Coaching is about seeing what shows up in the group and then using the appropriate tools.

6. **Do group goal setting.** The group has one topic; however, each member has an individual, measurable coaching goal.

7. **Do live on- the-spot coaching.** Generalize the lesson from one person to the entire group.

8. **Be keenly aware of opportunities to use the coaching skill of "making people right."** No judgment in front of peers.

9. **Establish group agreements or ground rules on confidentiality, conflict, and how the group operates.**

10. **Assign fieldwork and celebrate success.** Most important: Debrief. People learn from others' learning.

III. Building Virtual Relationships

IT'S ALL ABOUT CONNECTION.
The important thing to understand about virtual leadership, virtual coaching, and virtual relationships is this:

> *Leadership is about connection,*
> *not just physical presence.*

We know this based on our own experience. For example, think of times when you may have had to frequently call a coworker or vendor that you have never met. Sometimes you notice that when the relationship is good, you feel as if you really know this person, even though you have never seen them. That's the connection, but notice that it's based on the rapport, the connection in the relationship. Conversely, you can have a coworker or manager sitting right beside you, whom you talk to face-to-face, and you could still feel no rapport, no relationship.

So physical presence by itself is just one of the many factors in a relationship, but feeling connected is the key factor for effectiveness. For leaders this means that you want to take actions over the phone or through email that will help your staff feel:

- They are being heard;
- They are being supported;
- They are appreciated;
- They are understood;
- Their opinion is valued;
- They know you;
- They can count on you.

As leaders we accomplish all of the above virtually by how we use:

- Our tone of voice;
- The amount of time we spend on the phone with a person;
- How well we listen;
- Our choice of words in email;
- The types of questions we ask;
- How often we initiate the contact;
- The kinds of information we forward to people.

BUILDING VIRTUAL RELATIONSHIPS

If leaders want to strengthen the "connection" with virtual staff, they have to pay closer attention to the individual person and what that specific person needs to feel connected. Virtual relationships in general need more deliberate nurturing of the relationship. But once the connection is there and the relationship is nurtured and developed, a virtual relationship can be every bit as strong as a face-to-face relationship. Here are a few suggestions.

VIRTUAL RELATIONSHIP SUGGESTIONS

When you lead virtually, the skills for building relationships are somewhat different than in the traditional workplace. You need to be much better at figuring out other people's emotions without the usual visual clues of body language or behavior observation. You have to be better at building trust with minimal interaction. You also have to be able to demonstrate appreciation of people in new ways. Ask yourself:

- On a daily basis, what do you do to demonstrate to remote staff that they are not forgotten?

- Each time you speak with a direct report by phone, can you assess their morale? Their mood? What are they happy about? Concerned about?

- Do a self-evaluation on a scale of 1-10 (10 being the highest). How would each of your remote staff rate how much they trust you? What actions can you take to improve their trust in you?

IV. How to Make it Effortless

Virtual leadership is an advanced skill. It takes outstanding leadership skills and the willingness to really pay attention to what you are doing. However, virtual leadership can be effortless. How? By making it a lifestyle.

If you practice exceptional leadership in everything you do in all of your daily life, then virtual leadership becomes natural for you. For example, practice virtual leadership skills on the phone when ordering take out food; practice with co-workers when emailing about non-critical subjects; practice with that person on the telephone who is taking your catalog order. The idea is to become a leader all the time in every word you say, every action you take.

Have your leadership be so all-encompassing that it does not have to depend on face-to-face communication, so you can lead people under any circumstances.

And, most important, learn from your own experience. Get feedback from direct reports, peers and managers on how you are doing as a virtual leader. What works for them? What doesn't work? Make it your passion to become a master communicator, able to lead through phone, email, paper memo, or even just by reputation.

In short, the virtual leaders are those who learn to master virtual reality.

And as technology continues to expand, we have more to look forward to.

This is only the beginning ...

About the Author

Valerie Williams is an Executive Coach who runs her own business: Professional Coaching and Training, Inc. Val presents training seminars to organizations and also coaches people individually to achieve career and personal goals. She specializes in Leadership and Stress Management.

Val's experience includes several years as a Managed Health Care Executive at Prudential Insurance, managing staffs as large as 700 people. Val was Executive Director of Prucare, the HMO of Northern New Jersey; Director of Prucare Customer Service Operations for the Northeast Region; and Director of Group Underwriting, Prucare of New York. Val has managed an annual operating budget of over 25 million dollars with direct impact on a network of 500,000 insured patients and 8,000 physicians and hospital providers.

During her 13 years' experience at Prudential, Val managed several other areas, including Financial Services, Facilities Planning and Field Office Lease Negotiations.

Prior to her corporate career, Val worked with people on both physical and psychological rehab. Valerie earned a Bachelor of Science from Tufts University and a Master's Degree in Counseling Psychology from Boston University.

People throughout the United States, France, Finland, England and Australia work with Val to raise the quality of their professional lives. Val coaches people (often by telephone) to develop greater focus and overcome obstacles so they design the life they really want. In her seminars, Val is known for her interactive approach and practical style.

As a Coach, Val has presented seminars and coached executives and professionals at a variety of corporations, universities and professional organizations, including: Washington Mutual Bank, Premera Blue Cross, General Electric, Prudential, National Utility Investors, TIAA-CREF, American Express, Genentech, Pfizer, Harvard University, Pepsi, Nokia, University of Indianapolis, Horizon-Mercy HMO, AT&T, Lucent Technologies, Delta Dental, American Heart Association, Schering-Plough, ADP, Raytheon, Women Unlimited and more.

Val offers coaching in different formats: either individual coaching for executives or group coaching for several executives at once.

Val has been credentialed and awarded the designation "Master Certified Coach" by the International Coaching Federation.

Other Resources by Val Williams

TO ORDER
Visit our website: www.valwilliams.com
or Fax 877.443.4092

- ***Get the Best Out of Your People and Yourself:
  7 Practical Steps for Top Performance***
  This book gives 7 practical steps for leaders and
  executives who want to see top performance from
  the staff. The handbook gives excellent practical
  instructions on delegation, giving feedback,
  performance management, and coaching your
  people. 100 pages ($14.95 + $2 shipping)

- ***The Ways of Leadership*** (Audiotape)
  Strong Leadership is about more than what you
  "do." Real leadership is built on "who you are."
  ($10 + $1 shipping)

- ***Building Your Personal Foundation
  7 Steps for a Happier Life*** (Audiotape)
  Building your personal foundation will show you
  how to:
  - Raise your standards
  - Get your needs met
  - Eliminate what you tolerate
  - Restore integrity
  - Build boundaries
  - & more! ($10 + $1 shipping)

Shadowbrook Publishing
PO Box 2458, Edison NJ 08818
Fax 877.443.4092 • www.valwilliams.com

Share It With Others

If you'd like to order more books, you can fill out this form and fax it to us at (877) 443-4092, or visit our website to email us and see other products: www.valwilliams.com

QTY	Product	Price	Total
	Virtual Leadership	$	
	Sales Tax: (NJ residents add 6%)		
	Shipping/Handling (Add $2.00 per book)		
	Total		

Shipping Address

Name

Address 1

Address 2

City   State   Zip/Postal Code   Country

Phone   Fax

Email

Charge to:

Cardholder name: _____

Credit Card Number   (Circle one): Visa   Master Card   American Express

Expiration Date (MM/YY)

Fax completed order form to (877) 443-4092
If paying by check, mail check and completed form to:
Shadowbrook Publishing
PO Box 2458
Edison NJ 08818
Checks payable to Shadowbrook Publishing

Visit Val's website to see more products and services.